HR APPROVED WAYS TO TELL YOUR EMPLOYEES THEY ARE STUPID

Witty Alternatives for Those Things You Want to Say At Work But Can't

HEARTFUL PUBLISHING

Copyright © 2024 Heartful Publishing. All rights reserved.

Legal Notice

The content of this book is protected by copyright law. It is intended for personal use only. No part of this book may be reproduced, duplicated, transmitted, modified, distributed, sold, used, quoted, or paraphrased without the express written permission of the author or publisher. Any unauthorized use is strictly prohibited. The author and publisher accept no responsibility for any damages, reparations, or monetary losses arising from the use of the information contained in this book, whether directly or indirectly.

Disclaimer

The information provided in this book is for educational and entertainment purposes only. Every effort has been made to ensure the accuracy, reliability, and completeness of the information presented. However, no warranties, either express or implied, are made regarding the content. The author is not providing legal, financial, medical, or professional advice. Readers should consult with a licensed professional before attempting any techniques described in this book. By reading this book, the reader agrees that the author will not be liable for any losses or damages, direct or indirect, resulting from the use of the information contained herein, including but not limited to errors, omissions, or inaccuracies.

HR DISCLAIMER

Welcome to HR-Approved Ways to Tell Employees They're Stupid! Before we get started, let's set the record straight: this book is intended for comedic purposes only and should not be interpreted as a legitimate HR manual (our lawyers made sure we clarify that). While our amusing anecdotes and clever retorts may resonate with your daily office experiences, we don't recommend using them in real-life situations—Unless, of course, you're angling for a one-on-one with HR!. Think of this guide as a playful outlet for those thoughts that often linger in your mind but are best left unsaid.

Approach with humor, share a laugh, and keep in mind that our "politely informing" style is meant for amusement, not for professional growth.

Buckle up for some fun!

Attention: This is a blank page, much like my motivation after 3 PM!

What I Really Want To Say:

I'm so glad I can do your job and mine today. It's like a 2-for-1 deal!

HR Approved Alternative:

I'm always happy to support where needed

What I Really Want To Say:

Are you CC'ing the entire office because we need everyone's opinion on this, or...?

HR Approved Alternative:

Thanks for keeping everyone in the loop!

What I Really Want To Say:

Another meeting that could've been an email? Fantastic.

HR Approved Alternative:

I appreciate everyone taking the time to connect.

What I Really Want To Say:

I love getting last-minute requests—it's like a surprise party I never asked for

HR Approved Alternative:

Thanks for trusting me to help out with this on short notice!

What I Really Want To Say:

Oh, look, yet another 'urgent' request that wasn't urgent yesterday

HR Approved Alternative:

I'll prioritize that right away!

What I Really Want To Say: 🕶

Thanks for forwarding that email again—because I obviously didn't see it the first six times.

HR Approved Alternative:

Thank you for the reminder—I'll make sure it's on my radar.

What I Really Want To Say:

If brains were dynamite, yours wouldn't even blow your hat off.

HR Approved Alternative:

You have such a unique way of approaching things!

What I Really Want To Say:

Are you paid extra to be this dense?

HR Approved Alternative:

Wow, you're really exploring all angles here, aren't you?

What I Really Want To Say:

Could you try not being the worst today?

HR Approved Alternative:

I'd love to see you at your best today!

What I Really Want To Say:

Who hired you, and why are they still employed?

HR Approved Alternative:

You really bring your own flair to the team!

What I Really Want To Say:

I've seen rocks that think faster than you.

HR Approved Alternative:

Everyone has their own pace. Take all the time you need!

What I Really Want To Say:

Your incompetence is inspiring... to do things myself.

HR Approved Alternative:

You really encourage me to be proactive!

What I Really Want To Say:

Oh look, it's the reason we have 'mandatory' in meetings.

HR Approved Alternative:

Always great to have team-wide discussions!

What I Really Want To Say:

You bring a new level of 'why' to 'why are you here?

HR Approved Alternative:

I think your presence really makes a difference!

What I Really Want To Say: 🕶

If I wanted to hear nonsense, I'd let the office printer explain itself.

HR Approved Alternative:

It's always good to bounce ideas around!

What I Really Want To Say:

Any chance you're almost done being incompetent?

HR Approved Alternative:

How's the learning process going?

What I Really Want To Say:

If stupidity were an Olympic event, you'd medal

HR Approved Alternative:

Wow, you're really going for it today!

What I Really Want To Say:

Imagine understanding basic concepts... if only.

HR Approved Alternative:

I'd be happy to review the basics if that's helpful!

What I Really Want To Say:

Your input is as useful as a screen door on a submarine

HR Approved Alternative:

I appreciate your unique perspective

What I Really Want To Say:

Oh, are we pretending to be useful today?

HR Approved Alternative:

It's always nice to see people give their all!

What I Really Want To Say:

You have the efficiency of a one-legged sloth

HR Approved Alternative:

You definitely take your time—no rush!

What I Really Want To Say:

Your emails are a journey through nonsense.

HR Approved Alternative:

Let's keep communications as clear as possible!

What I Really Want To Say:

Why use common sense when you have... whatever that is

HR Approved Alternative:

You have such a fresh approach to problem-solving!

What I Really Want To Say:

I bet your idea of multitasking is chewing gum and walking.

HR Approved Alternative:

You know, there's nothing wrong with focus!

What I Really Want To Say:

You have all the charisma of expired yogurt.

HR Approved Alternative:

You have a very unique energy

What I Really Want To Say:

Your ideas make me feel like I'm losing brain cells.

HR Approved Alternative:

That's definitely one way to think about it!

What I Really Want To Say:

Are you here to lower the IQ of the whole department?

HR Approved Alternative:

I'm sure you'll bring some fresh ideas to the team!

What I Really Want To Say:

You could make coffee nervous

HR Approved Alternative:

Your energy really keeps the place lively!

What I Really Want To Say:

If only you could put as much effort into thinking as you do into existing.

HR Approved Alternative:

You have such a presence on the team!

What I Really Want To Say:

If there were an award for wasting time, you'd be the world champ.

HR Approved Alternative:

You definitely keep us all grounded in reality!

What I Really Want To Say:

If common sense was currency, you'd be bankrupt.

HR Approved Alternative:

Your unique insights are definitely refreshing!

What I Really Want To Say:

Please don't let common sense get in the way of your process.

HR Approved Alternative:

I appreciate your alternative take on things!

What I Really Want To Say:

Did you lose a bet that forced you into this job?

HR Approved Alternative:

Everyone finds their calling eventually!

What I Really Want To Say:

You're about as reliable as a broken clock.

HR Approved Alternative:

Consistency is definitely key in this role!

What I Really Want To Say:

You're like a black hole for productivity.

HR Approved Alternative:

I think you add a lot to team morale!

What I Really Want To Say:

Did you skip the meeting, or are you just pretending not to know?

HR Approved Alternative:

I can fill you in on the key points if that would help!

What I Really Want To Say:

That idea should have stayed in drafts

HR Approved Alternative:

Let's brainstorm a little more on this!

What I Really Want To Say:

Your email brought me to the edge of sanity. Impressive

HR Approved Alternative:

Thanks for the detailed message. I'll review it carefully!

What I Really Want To Say:

Let me guess, you just skimmed that report, right?

HR Approved Alternative:

It might help to take a closer look at page 3

What I Really Want To Say:

The bar was low, but you found a way to limbo under it

HR Approved Alternative:

It's nice to see you bringing your unique perspective!

What I Really Want To Say:

Nothing says 'team player' like watching us struggle while you do nothing.

HR Approved Alternative:

If you're looking for ways to contribute, I have a few ideas!

What I Really Want To Say:

I love how you ask questions that we just covered.

HR Approved Alternative:

I'm happy to recap that part for you!

What I Really Want To Say:

Congratulations on making everything harder for everyone else.

HR Approved Alternative:

It's always good to have a new perspective in the mix!

What I Really Want To Say:

Are you here to work, or just for the free coffee?

HR Approved Alternative:

You really seem to appreciate our amenities!

What I Really Want To Say:

Did you read that email or just skim the title?

HR Approved Alternative:

Let me know if you need more details on the email!

What I Really Want To Say:

Oh, you're not late. You're just on-brand late

HR Approved Alternative:

It's good to see you! We've saved a spot for you.

What I Really Want To Say:

Nothing like seeing your half-finished work to brighten my day.

HR Approved Alternative:

Let's collaborate to finish this strong!

What I Really Want To Say:

I'd say 'think outside the box,' but you still haven't found the box

HR Approved Alternative:

Let's explore a few more ideas together!

What I Really Want To Say:

It's amazing how 'urgent' doesn't seem to mean anything to you

HR Approved Alternative:

Just a friendly reminder on that deadline!

What I Really Want To Say:

Are you even pretending to care, or is this for real?

HR Approved Alternative:

I'd love to get your buy-in on this project!

What I Really Want To Say:

Great job on making that meeting five times longer than it needed to be

HR Approved Alternative:

Thanks for the thorough discussion!

What I Really Want To Say:

Oh, perfect, another 'reply all' email from you.

HR Approved Alternative:

Just a reminder that we can keep this to direct replies!

What I Really Want To Say:

Impressive work ignoring every instruction in that email!

HR Approved Alternative:

If any part of the email was unclear, feel free to ask!

What I Really Want To Say:

Do you have a timer to ensure you're exactly 5 minutes late to everything?

HR Approved Alternative:

Great to have you here, as always!

What I Really Want To Say:

Oh, that's a fantastic idea... if we want it to fail.

HR Approved Alternative:

We might need to refine that approach a bit!

What I Really Want To Say:

I've never seen someone misunderstand instructions so creatively.

HR Approved Alternative:

Your interpretation is unique—let's discuss

What I Really Want To Say:

Do you ever try working instead of just talking about it?

HR Approved Alternative:

I'd love to see your follow-through on this!

What I Really Want To Say:

Oh, that's going to be your problem, not mine.

HR Approved Alternative:

I'll let you take the lead on this one!

What I Really Want To Say:

You work harder at avoiding work than actually doing it

HR Approved Alternative:

You have a very unique approach to prioritizing!

What I Really Want To Say:

Thank you for contributing absolutely nothing to that project.

HR Approved Alternative:

It's great to have everyone's participation in some way!

What I Really Want To Say:

Can't wait to hear your 'helpful' feedback that's mostly complaints

HR Approved Alternative:

I know you have some valuable insights to share!

What I Really Want To Say:

I didn't know human sloths existed until I met you

HR Approved Alternative:

Everyone's pace is different, and that's okay!

What I Really Want To Say:

Is your goal to make our job harder?

HR Approved Alternative:

We all enjoy a challenge now and then!

What I Really Want To Say:

I hope 'underperforming' isn't your main skill set.

HR Approved Alternative:

You bring such a balanced, calm energy!

What I Really Want To Say:

That's a fascinating way to avoid any real responsibility.

HR Approved Alternative:

You're so flexible with your approach to projects!

What I Really Want To Say:

Wow, it's like you get paid to ignore emails

HR Approved Alternative:

Let me know if any messages aren't reaching you!

What I Really Want To Say:

That idea? Let's just say, we're not aiming for 'worst-ever' status.

HR Approved Alternative:

Every idea contributes to the creative process!

What I Really Want To Say:

Wow, another 30-minute speech with no clear point

HR Approved Alternative:

You're always so enthusiastic in meetings!

What I Really Want To Say:

What would we do without your...enthusiastic chaos?

HR Approved Alternative:

You definitely add a lot of energy to our team!

What I Really Want To Say:

For someone so quiet in meetings, you're oddly loud in emails.

HR Approved Alternative:

Your written thoughts are always so detailed!

Printed in Great Britain
by Amazon